Dream Gardens
Across America

WILEY

John Wiley & Sons, Inc.

Better Homes and Gardens® Dream Gardens Across America
Contributing Project Editor: Renee Freemon Mulvihill
Contributing Designer: Cathy Brett
Editor, Garden Books: Denny Schrock
Editorial Assistant: Heather Knowles
Contributing Copy Editor: Terri Fredrickson
Contributing Proofreaders: Fran Gardner, Peg Smith
Contributing Indexer: Ellen Sherron

Meredith® Books
Editorial Director: Gregory H. Kayko
Editor in Chief, Garden: Doug Jimerson
Editorial Manager: David Speer
Art Director: Tim Alexander
Managing Editor: Doug Kouma
Executive Director, Sales: Ken Zagor
Director, Operations: George A. Susral
Director, Production: Douglas M. Johnston
Business Director: Janice Croat
Imaging Center Operator: Tony Jungweber

John Wiley & Sons, Inc.
Publisher: Natalie Chapman
Associate Publisher: Jessica Goodman
Executive Editor: Anne Ficklen
Assistant Editor: Charleen Barila
Production Director: Diana Cisek
Manufacturing Manager: Tom Hyland

Better Homes and Gardens Magazine
Editor in Chief: Gayle Goodson Butler

Meredith Publishing Group
President: Tom Harty
Excutive Vice President: Doug Olson

Meredith Corporation
Chairman of the Board: William T. Kerr
President and Chief Executive Officer: Stephen M. Lacy

In Memoriam: E.T. Meredith III (1933–2003)

This book is printed on acid-free paper.
Copyright © 2010 by Meredith Corporation, Des Moines, IA.
All rights reserved
Published by John Wiley & Sons, Inc., Hoboken, New Jersey
Published simultaneously in Canada

Note to Reader: Due to differing conditions, tools, and individual skills, Meredith Corporation assumes no responsibility for any damages, injuries suffered, or losses incurred as a result of following the information published in this book. Before beginning any project, review the instructions carefully and, if any doubts or questions remain, consult local experts or authorities. Because codes and regulations vary greatly, you should always check with authorities to ensure that your project complies with all applicable local codes and regulations. Always read and observe all the safety precautions provided by manufacturers of any tools, equipment, or supplies, and follow all accepted safety procedures.

For general information on our other products and services or for technical support, please contact our Customer Care Department within the United States at (800) 762-2974, outside the United States at (317) 572-3993 or fax (317) 572-4002.
Wiley also publishes its books in a variety of electronic formats. Some content that appears in print may not be available in electronic books.
For more information about Wiley products, visit our web site at www.wiley.com.

Library of Congress Cataloging-in-Publication Data

LOC information available upon request.
ISBN 978-0-470-87843-9 (paper)

Printed in the United States of America

10 9 8 7 6 5 4 3 2 1

contents

Chapter 7 Asian Influence

Chapter 8 Backyard Retreats

Chapter 9 Cottage Style

floral fantasies

Overflowing with beautiful
blooms, these gardens
enchant the senses with rich
color and delightful fragrance.
Take a moment to linger
among the flowers.

This photo: A river of 6,000 pastel tulips winds its way through the front yard of this charming brick cottage. Newly planted every fall to ensure a grand show, the tulip display is in its prime for a couple of weeks in early May. *Right:* A skirt of dainty violets grows along the front edge of all beds to cover up the tulips' gangly legs.

tulip time

Flower power rules in this garden, where 8,000 tulips greet spring.

There is no space to tiptoe through the tulips in this Pennsylvania garden. There are simply too many flowers. Thousands of bulbs in a rainbow of hues are planted cheek by jowl to create a scene that slows passing traffic for weeks each spring. Add a few spring beauties to your garden with these simple tulip-growing tips.

■ Plan ahead. Tulips and other spring-flowering bulbs must be planted in fall. Plan and plant in autumn for next year's display. First, select a planting site. Tulips thrive in full sun and well-drained soil. Avoid moist or soggy sites; the bulbs will rot. Mail-order bulb companies often offer the largest selection and highest quality bulbs. Place your order in summer for fall delivery.

■ Plant smart. Plant tulips at least 8 inches deep in October or November. Place each bulb in the planting hole so the pointed side is up. Feed bulbs with a bulb-booster fertilizer, and top the planting with a ½-inch layer of mulch. Tulips require a chilling period in winter to bloom the next spring. If you live in a region with warm winters, make sure to plant prechilled bulbs.

This photo: Dangling from a tree, this hanging basket features a cloud of white verbena punctuated with bright white petunias. Blooming baskets such as this are prolific at garden centers in spring. Purchase your favorites, and enjoy a colorful show long after the tulips are gone. *Left:* Nestled in natural wood planters and baskets, flowering plants, such as this pink azalea, seamlessly blend into the beds of color-rich tulips.

variations on a theme

A garden composed around a single kind of flower doesn't have to be a one-note wonder. Variations and accents used to perfection can turn that single theme into high art.

Artistic accents like this bunny sculpture or companion plantings like the clematis growing through the white picket fence enrich the tone and provide a counterpoint to the main floral theme—hydrangeas—in this Georgia landscape.

One-note wonder. One-trick pony. One-night stand. None of these phrases should describe your garden, even if it is based on a single type of flower.

So what are you to do if you've fallen in love with roses or daylilies or tulips or hydrangeas? Transform your single-flower garden from one to wonderful with a few easy tips.

■ Don't be rigid about staying single. Include as many of your favorites as you wish, but let some variety sneak in. Find other plants that are good companions to your chosen flower, and weave them into the texture of your garden like gold thread through a tapestry.

■ Use containers, furniture, and garden art as accents. Choose colors that complement your favorite flowers, as the blue and white accents in this garden complement the hydrangeas.

Right: A white arbor overrun by vines and flanked by two fierce-looking rabbits provides the perfect counterpoint to the soccer ball-size blooms of 'Annabelle' hydrangeas. Use arbors, trellises, and other architectural elements to add height to a garden dominated by less lofty plants. *Below:* Highlight your favorite plants by putting some in unexpected places. This pink 'Penny Mac' hydrangea, which you would expect to find planted in the ground, sits happily in a wood box.

Left: Ferns and astilbes are perfect planting partners to protect these prize-winning hydrangeas from the hot Southern sun. Pick companion plants for their growing characteristics as well as their color, texture, and size. *Right:* Purple hydrangeas fill a large bed in front of this charming gazebo. It's hard to go over the top when you're concentrating on a single type of flower. Plant your favorites to emphasize their exuberance and your enthusiasm for them. *Below:* If you've decided to have a garden built around a single flower, remember to use lots of it. Even hydrangeas, which seem at first glance to be all pretty much the same, display a variety of shapes, sizes, and colors.

time for
a garden

Grow a great garden and
have time to enjoy it too,
with tips from this low-
maintenance wonder.

This photo: Low-maintenance and easy-care flowers, such as spider flower (*Cleome* spp.), shrub roses, and daylilies, bloom from early summer to frost. *Right:* Yellow 'Stella d'Oro' daylilies light the garden by day, and simple solar lamps, found at garden centers, cast a pretty glow at night.

Overflowing flower borders, neatly painted picket fences, and a bold backyard waterfall make this Missouri garden a showplace. The secret behind the blooming success is planning for a low-maintenance landscape. This piece of paradise is proof that you don't have to dedicate hours every week to planting, weeding, and watering to enjoy a colorful outdoor oasis. Borrow a few of these ideas and begin transforming your garden into a low-care wonder.

■ Make smart plant choices. Each plant species is unique. Some need to be coaxed and coddled into blooming and thriving in your garden while others will send up blossom after blossom with little help from you. A garden that receives at least 8 hours of sun a day and has well-drained soil will host many easy-care plants, including purple coneflower (*Echinacea purpurea)*, stonecrop (*Sedum* spp.), daylily (*Hemerocallis* spp.), ornamental grass (such as *Miscanthus* spp.), and many cultivars of shrub roses. For a shade garden, opt for hostas, ferns, fringed bleeding heart (*Dicentra eximia)*, and spotted deadnettle (*Lamium maculatum)*.

Above: A valuable investment, the mortared brick walkway pays returns in long-lasting good looks and a carefree nature. *Right:* A butterfly bush anchors one side of the flagstone path while magenta shrub roses flourish on the other side.

This photo: Perennials planted cheek by jowl bloom in chorus with the splashing waterfall. An excellent landscape solution for a slope, the waterfall provides pleasing music to the seating area near the house. *Right:* Colorful fish and water lilies are right at home in the calm water in the pond below the waterfall.

■ Thwart weeds before they become a problem. Control begins at planting time. Granular weed-and-feed products that prevent weeds from germinating must be applied before they emerge. Also, a 2- to 3-inch layer of organic mulch, such as shredded bark, creates an effective barrier against weeds and adds valuable nutrients to the soil as it breaks down.

■ Fill gaps with colorful annuals. Some perennials or shrubs may not return as expected after a rough winter. Add instant color where they once grew by planting annuals. Long-blooming annuals will add to the lush feel of the garden and prevent weeds while giving you time to select a new perennial or shrub for the space.

planting by nature

Simple multiplication adds to the abundance of this Canadian garden. A committee of self-sowing plants blankets the beds with fruitful seeds for an ongoing show of color.

Above: Golden ninebark *(Physocarpus opulifolius)* and *Potentilla* 'Yellow Gem' create a color frame. *Right:* A cast of shrubs and small trees supports the swaths of color that curl through this garden. These woody plants form an ever-present framework for the mounds of annuals and perennials. *Potentilla* 'Yellow Gem' blooms in the foreground, while spiky Adam's needle *(Yucca filamentosa)* adds texture in the back.

Most of the planting in this sprawling garden is left to Mother Nature. One look at the scene she magically paints year after year and you'll sing praises of her planting panache.

A host of self-seeding plants that thrive in the rigors of this Canadian province makes growing great gardens a doable feat. Punctuated by showy lilies and shrubs with pleasing textures, the self-seeding plants form drifts of color throughout the growing season. Aside from occasional deadheading of spent blooms and vigilant plucking out of unwanted seedlings by the gardener, Mother Nature takes care of the planting and growing. Encourage self-seeding plants to populate your garden with these simple tips.

■ Search out desirable self-seeding plants. Not all plants self-seed; talk with fellow gardeners to learn which plants self-seed in your area. Be skeptical of vigorous self-seeders and those plants whose seedlings are difficult to eradicate. These plants can quickly become garden thugs, choking out nearby pleasing plants.

■ Discontinue deadheading about a month before the first frost to give seeds time to fully develop before winter arrives. Allow plants to remain standing in the garden through winter to encourage seeds to disperse.

■ Create a good seedbed around self-seeding plants by leaving the soil exposed. Mulch and dense groundcovers will discourage seed from rooting. For early spring, plant bulbs that naturalize, such as daffodils.

Left: Soaring red Maltese cross *(Lychnis chalcedonica),* silver lamb's ears *(Stachys byzantina),* peach-leaf bellflower *(Campanula persicifolia),* and chartreuse lady's mantle *(Alchemilla mollis)* all self-seed freely, planting themselves wherever wind or animals transport their seed. *Above right:* The fluffy silver seedheads of *Clematis integrifolia* are just as lovely as the nodding purple flowers of this climbing plant. Train it onto a tripod or obelisk, or twine it through perennial plantings. *Right:* Candles of brilliant purple *Veronica spicata* rise behind a stand of violas and a sea of woolly thyme *(Thymus pseudolanuginosus).*

Left: The curled petals of this Turk's cap lily contrast with the star-shape Asiatic lily flowers that decorate the garden. Lilies have an impressive presence in the garden for a month or more, from the time their buds expand to when their petals fall. **Below:** Purple *Veronica spicata* borders a vista of a rose-clad arbor. Wands of blue *Campanula* dance behind the *Veronica,* and frothy white plums of meadowsweet *(Filipendula purpurea* f. *albiflora)* stand to the left. This lush, attractive look is maintained by regular culling of unwanted seedlings. Pluck weak seedlings and those that have populated an area in prolific numbers every few weeks.

Right: *Veronica spicata* and peach-pink Asiatic lilies are a striking couple. Self-seeding can create color combinations that would not normally occur in a planned garden. Stand back and watch nature at work!

fields of color

A cut-flower farm, this lush Oregon garden is flush with floral inspiration for months of petal-packed color.

Sweetgum trees *(Liquidambar styraciflua)* and more than 20 varieties of rambling roses line the gravel drive with pleasing form and fragrance.

Continuous bloom is the livelihood of this working cut-flower farm. Perched on a bank of the Willamette River in Newberg, Oregon, the home and gardens bask in nearly perfect growing conditions. Well-drained soil, mild winters, and a Zone 8 climate make growing great plants relatively simple. Even the best gardening climate doesn't ensure months of nonstop flower color, though. Continuous bloom calls for thoughtful planning and a little research. Add weeks of flower power to your garden with these tips.

■ Get out and see gardens in your area. The best way to learn about what will thrive in your growing zone is to visit nearby gardens. Your neighbors' plots, botanical gardens, university trial gardens, and public garden spaces are all sources of inspiration. Learn more by attending local symposiums and garden get-togethers. Check with your county extension office about Master Gardener classes.

■ Don't forget about trees and shrubs. Beautiful garden color isn't limited to annuals and perennials. Flowering trees and shrubs offer bountiful springtime color options. Rhododendrons, azaleas, witch hazels, crabapples, dogwoods, and magnolias are just a few of the many flowering woody plants. Many boast fantastic fall color in addition to their spring show.

■ Take notes. Building a continuously blooming garden is a multiyear endeavor. Each year you'll add plants, filling gaps in flowering times and extending the season. Using a pencil and paper or a camera, note what blooms in your garden each week. Put the findings to work by searching out plants to complement your space.

rooms with blooms

Perfume-rich climbing roses, lush stands of boxwood and laurel, and rustic brick paths divvy up a simple suburban backyard into a series of intimate garden rooms.

Above: Asiatic lilies (*Lilium* spp.), blooming althaea *(Althaea cannabina)*, and sculptural bear's breeches *(Acanthus spinosus)* create a dense, color-rich living screen to separate the shady pergola sitting area from the bright and sunny brick patio. Although the lilies will drop their blooms, the althaea and bear's breeches will display colorful petals for most of the summer. *Left:* A clematis-clad pergola borders one side of the home and reveals lovely views of the garden beyond. A brick path extending from the pergola leads visitors to a garden swing across the way and, along with the paired boxwood hedges *(Buxus sempervirens)*, visually divides areas of the garden.

Designing a garden is similar to drawing up plans for a house. Just as you plan spaces for certain tasks, such as a kitchen for preparing meals and a bedroom for sleeping, your garden has rooms too. Create an outdoor dining room beyond your back door, or group comfy Adirondack chairs with a side table or two for a cozy outdoor living room.

In the garden, dense green hedges and blossoming stands of flowers become walls; vibrant green grass, pebbles, and chunks of stone make floors; and a rich, blue sky makes a never-ending ceiling.

Building outdoor rooms begins with delineating the space. A sprawling backyard can become an intimate oasis with well-placed plants, structures, and paths.

■ Add structures. Use fences, pergolas, and walls to define spaces. White picket fences cloaked with fragrant roses define the edges of several flower-filled rooms in this garden. On the far side of the property, a white pergola, complete with a double swing, provides a quiet nook for reading and relaxing.

■ Plant living screens. Tall and short hedges and clumps of flowering perennials form lovely walls that change with the seasons.

■ Lay paths. A simple pebble path or a complex brick or stone walkway can easily separate areas at ground level while leading visitors from one garden room to another. For a more intimate setting, pair a path with a living screen.

Above left: 'Simplicity' roses soften a white picket fence and form a boundary on one side of the garden. *Left:* Antique black urns planted with *Dracaenas* denote the entrance to the patio and dining area beyond. *Right:* Bold Asiatic lilies, clusters of white phlox *(Phlox paniculata)*, lacy burgundy leaves of Japanese maple *(Acer palmatum)*, and airy wands of *Verbena bonariensis* all boast eye-pleasing texture. United by a color palette rich in magenta, red, purple, and shades of green, this garden shows its warm and soothing personality.

country charm

Whether they're part of a large acreage or a small suburban lot, these country gardens show off a carefree attitude and welcoming spirit. Just step inside and you'll feel right at home.

This photo: A picket fence surrounds a garden filled with annuals, perennials, and shrubs. Once home to vegetables exclusively, the garden now boasts blooms all summer. *Left:* Single hollyhocks pop up throughout the garden in serendipitous combinations.

all in the family

Annuals, perennials, conifers, flowering shrubs, and trees all have a place in this country garden on the coast of Maine.

There are no rules in garden design. Simply plant what makes your heart sing and you'll be pleased with the results. This 3-acre garden in Northport, Maine, is a spectacular show of spring-to-summer blooms thanks to plant combinations the owner chose because she loved the plants when she saw them at the garden center. The next time you are combining plants, consider these design ideas.

■ Take advantage of contrasting textures. In shade gardens, *Rodgersia*, with its rough, handsome leaves, grows alongside *Epimedium*, whose fanciful heart-shape foliage seems to float on delicate stems. The contrasting textures highlight the unique attributes of each plant. Trees and shrubs with interesting bark also play up pleasing textures in the garden. Paperbark maple (*Acer griseum*), river birch (*Betula nigra*), and shagbark hickory (*Carya ovata*) all boast peeling bark.

■ Remember foliage color. For contrast, juxtapose a plant with green or red foliage with another that has variegated leaves. Be careful; too much variegated foliage can overwhelm a small space. Blue-green foliage and chartreuse make another pleasing combination.

■ Let Mother Nature do the planting. Allow your favorite self-seeding plants to pop up throughout the garden. Often you'll be pleased with the effortless outcome. Hollyhocks and columbine ramble around this garden and make good companions for all the other plants. When they grow where they are not wanted, delicate roots make seedlings easy to pluck out of the soil.

country
in the city

A charming garden shed with rustic appeal takes center stage in this urban backyard.

Above: **A cottage garden filled with spider flowers and zinnias skirts the shed with carefree color. Annuals like these self-seed for beauty year after year.** *Left:* **A plush chair and a bistro table make this garden house a destination that is difficult to leave.**

Call it whatever you like—a garden shed, garden house, home office, guesthouse, playhouse—a building set in a garden can fill many roles. Aside from its numerous interior functions, a thoughtfully designed shed adds abundant character and interest to an outdoor oasis. Situated in the middle of an urban development in northeastern Ohio, this rough cedar shed gives the backyard a decidedly country feel in the middle of glass-and-steel buildings.

The first step toward building your garden shed is to define how you will use the space. The possibilities are almost endless. Here are a few of the most popular ways to use these charming backyard structures.

■ A storage place for garden gear. Keep your trowels, rakes, garden gloves, wheelbarrow, and potting supplies in one convenient place. Depending on what you would like to store inside it, a garden shed does not have to be large. A 5-foot-square structure provides ample space for

tools. Would you like to store your lawn mower in the shed too? How about creating a convenient place for potting containers? Opt for a shed that is at least 8×10 feet.

■ A backyard gathering spot. The shed pictured here is a backyard retreat complete with comfy chairs, a table for dining, and a funky chandelier. The screened windows make it a cool place to gather on hot summer nights as breezes blow through yet bugs are kept out.

■ A home office. Becoming popular in temperate climates where heating and cooling are not an issue, a backyard office offers solitude in the midst of a lush setting. Plus, you can shut the door on your work and go inside your house at the end of the day. Tomorrow's tasks will be neatly hidden away until you return to your garden office the following day.

Above: **Lots of windows saturate the shed with light and contribute to its inviting countenance. Valuable on hot summer nights, the screened windows can be opened to cool the shed while keeping bugs at bay.** *Right:* **A lime green hosta and chartreuse sweet potato vine light up multihued croton, a common houseplant.**

just right

Strengths and weaknesses—every yard has them. Assessing your own growing conditions and needs will help you plan a garden that's tailor-made to thrive.

This photo: A white picket fence and a plethora of petunias, snapdragons, and ornamental sweet potato vine *(Ipomoea batatas)* give the front of this home a cottage feel. *Right:* This gazebo-like bird feeder rises amid Russian sage *(Perovskia* spp.) and purple coneflowers *(Echinacea purpurea)* in the backyard.

Sunny or shaded, warm or cold, large or small. Gardens all have unique characteristics that can influence the way you plan and tend your backyard haven. Identifying the best—and worst—parts of your space will help you decide what kind of garden will work best. Sometimes it even gives you ideas you wouldn't have thought of otherwise. In this Minnesota garden, an array of factors guided the homeowners' choice of flowers and structures. Identify strengths and weaknesses in your yard with these tips.

■ Research what will grow best in your garden. It sounds simple, but there are many things to consider. How much sunlight does the space receive? What are the temperatures around your house? Thinking about these elements while choosing flowers and plants will guide you toward a naturally thriving garden. In this garden, for example, the front yard receives full sun, which makes cottage-garden flowers natural choices. They include Arkansas rose

(*Rosa arkansana*), *Phlox paniculata* hybrids, snapdragons (*Antirrhinum majus*), petunias, and purple obedient plant (*Physostegia virginiana*). Visit local nurseries and read gardening materials to find out more about your area and its growing conditions.

■ Observe how your garden develops. As plants and flowers grow, the character of your garden also begins to bloom. In this garden's case, the homeowners noticed an increase in birds. They responded to this new characteristic by encouraging the feathered friends to stick around. Two birdbaths, five birdhouses, and 10 feeders make the birds feel right at home. If you like to provide food for birds, choose thistle for small ones and a grain/sunflower mix for large birds.

■ Consider what you need to enjoy gardening. Instead of searching fruitlessly in your garage for gardening tools, keep them organized so you can get straight to tending flowers. Something as simple as devoting a corner of your garage or basement to your gardening materials will ensure everything has a space. This garden includes a 5×7-foot shed. Although it's small, the shed keeps everything garden-related close at hand.

vintage treasures

A mix of collectibles and colorful perennials creates a garden planted straight from the heart.

Left: Annuals planted in matching blue containers dress up the front steps and extend the urban lot's limited garden space.

Above: The ivy-covered 1886 Victorian home forms an ideal backdrop for a storybook garden. Pink roses near the arbor greet visitors with a splash of color.

Who says urban gardens can't have quaint, country charm? A wealth of flea market finds and colorful containers, combined with tightly packed perennials and flourishing vines, brings a welcoming, down-home feel to this compact Chicago lot. Take a cue from this exuberant landscape and find out how to fill even the smallest spaces with maximum character. All it takes is a little creativity.

■ Collect what you love—and then figure out where to use it. Always start with a rough plan, but never be afraid to bring home plants that catch your eye. If you supplement your basic garden plan with these newfound favorites, you can add unexpected charm to unfilled corners or containers. Similarly, pieces of architectural ironwork or a collection of rustic birdhouses can add another layer of interest to garden beds and give the space unique personality.

Above: **Climbing vines, containers, and garden ornaments frame the potting shed doorway.** *Right:* **Texture and foliage, accented by annuals in containers, create interest in shady areas. Stepping-stones—surrounded by sweet woodruff (*Galium odoratum*) in shade and sedum in sunny patches—form informal pathways.**

Left: **A fence provides a decorative boundary for the Chicago garden. Inside the fence, perennials supplemented by annuals bring continuous color.** *Above:* **Containers and flea market finds lend extra drama when grouped. The blue containers in this display and throughout the garden create a cohesive look.**

■ Think vertically. When space is limited, look to vines to add welcome color and flower power. In this garden, a mix of annual and perennial climbers, such as morning glory *(Ipomoea purpurea)*, porcelain berry vine *(Ampelopsis brevipedunculata)*, and climbing roses, scramble up trellises and arbors. Although floppy flowers are often a popular feature in cottage gardens, staking plants helps them grow tall and straight—so you can fit more of your favorites into a small bed.

■ Group items for impact. A handful of collectibles artistically arranged can serve as a welcome landing point for the eye amid a showcase of blooms. On this front porch, containers in striking blue hues gently lead visitors to the front door and seamlessly connect the home and garden.

cozy casual

This Wisconsin garden proves that any
backyard can be a free-flowing retreat.

This photo: A cattail fountain surrounded by flowers and a tall arched trellis serves as the garden's centerpiece. The fountain shoots water from the tops of the cattails, mimicking the arch of the trellis entwined with honeysuckle vines.
Right: A birdhouse adds a quaint touch to the garden. Phlox, yarrow, purple coneflowers, and ligularia surround it with soft color.

The reasons for having a garden are plentiful and range from the satisfaction of designing and planting to the peaceful appreciation of watching your hard work grow. One reason that ranks high on the list: creating a welcoming spot for visitors. This garden is an inviting space. The plantings create a meandering path where visitors can see flowers at varying heights, and the loose spacing between varieties makes the garden visually open. Take a few cues from this garden to design your welcoming atmosphere.

■ Let go of your inner perfectionist. If you like the country-garden look, step back and let plants do their thing once in a while. In this garden, that means fronds hang over into the walkways. The result is a natural look that's not overly manicured.

This photo: The garden house is tucked among the numerous flowers and plants. A grand weeping willow hangs over it, helping it blend with its surroundings. *Right:* A large fence keeps animals out but invites visitors into the peaceful garden. The garden isn't constricted by the fence; planters near and on the gate offer a preview of the plants inside.

■ Keep it simple. To achieve a garden with cottage appeal, consider fewer blooms, and space them out. Select varieties are sprinkled throughout this garden and, with fewer flowers competing for attention, the colors pop against the greenery.

■ Consider the design of your fence. Pesky animals can make fencing your garden a necessity. However, some fences are more inviting than others. Look for designs with openings so neighbors and passersby can enjoy views of your garden. This fence was designed to keep deer out; if small animals are nuisances in your garden, choose a fence with small, but more plentiful, openings.

shaded sanctuaries

Boldly embrace the wide array of plants that will thrive in shaded spaces. Take a look at how these gardens blend bright color, striking form, and distinctive texture.

sweet
serenity

A soothing color palette makes this Alabama garden a peaceful oasis for all who visit.

This photo: Young fronds of ostrich fern *(Matteuccia struthiopteris)* unfurl in the spring. *Right:* The arched doorways of the pavilion lend it an Old World look. Climbing roses scramble up the roofline, subtly giving the structure less severe angles.

Like people, gardens have personalities. Is your garden boisterous and invigorating? Or quiet and calming? Rooted in serenity, this shaded retreat inspires contemplative relaxation. From the placement of landscape features to plant selection, the garden encourages visitors to toss away their troubles and revel in the simple beauty of nature. Here's how to craft a similar space to come home to at the end of the day.

■ Choose a simple, calm color scheme. Warm hues, such as red, orange, and yellow, add energy; cool colors, such as green, blue, and purple, bring about a quiet state of mind. Green is the primary color of this garden. Accented with white and a dash of pastel hues here and there, the Alabama garden is full of interest even with a limited color palette.

Above: **Earth-hue stone on the facade of the house and in the garden creates a seamless transition from home to landscape.** *Right:* **A simple stone path draws visitors into the woodland garden, which is softly colored with pastel foxgloves.**

Above: **Shape and texture reign supreme along this walkway. Neatly clipped boxwoods and sprawling ivy form tasteful groundcover.** *Left:* **The soothing sound of falling water permeates the house and garden thanks to a large fountain.**

When planning your garden, consider emphasizing just one hue. A monochromatic color scheme is particularly effective when multiple shades of one color are planted together. Pastels are popular and effective choices, but bold colors can be suitable when used with taste and restraint.

■ Create garden retreats. A thoughtfully placed bench near a reflecting pool or a pergola situated near the house for easy alfresco dining encourages you to slow down and enjoy the space. Garden seating does not have to be expensive or complicated. A smooth stump or a flat rock can be an impromptu chair.

■ Engage the senses. Running water, eye-pleasing vistas, and sweet fragrance will all enhance your garden retreat. When you are fully immersed in a space, it's easy to cast your cares aside.

shady characters

Make your woodland garden a shade brighter by incorporating a wonderfully diverse palette of plants that require minimal sun.

Right: This shady entrance border stretches three tiers deep down the slope that leads to a log home nestled among tall conifers in the Pacific Northwest. Variegated English boxwood and yellow shrub dogwoods brighten the area, which features rustic stepping-stones marking a path to an arbor-covered staircase. *Above:* This Japanese maple—*Acer palmatum* 'Beni schichihenge'—features luscious orange-pink leaves, which are dazzling in the shade. The small, twiggy trees grow only 6 feet tall.

L Life in a woodland clearing surrounded by tall conifers provides plenty of peace and quiet, plus a whole lot of shade—so much shade that some homeowners think a garden plan could never see the light of day. How wrong they are. Follow these guidelines for a color-filled plot overflowing with shade-loving plants that can be as close as your front yard.

■ Start by planting bright-blooming rhododendrons under mature evergreens, then add azaleas and small woodland plants—trilliums, epimediums, ferns, anemones, and some bulbs.

■ Bridge the gap between 80- to 100-foot-tall firs and 1-gallon rhododendrons with understory trees. Small maples fill that role in this garden. The budget-savvy homeowners bought tiny trees, which aren't prone to setback shock and will catch up with bigger trees in just a few seasons.

■ Make an entrance. Follow the example of these homeowners, who converted a dry, weedy, sandy slope into a welcoming entry garden. First, the area was terraced with rocks, then a fence and arbor—inspired by the rustic log home to which they lead—were added. Laburnum was draped over the arbor as a crowning touch. Now visitors follow a stepping-stone path through lush foliage to a serene staircase that culminates at the house.

■ Add complementary color. This garden features chartreuse and burgundy, which pop out from the mild green of the surrounding evergreens. Variegated grasses, primroses, winter hazel, dogwood, barberry, and yellow locust are all great choices to brighten a shade garden.

Above left: Purple 'Negrita' tulips and a golden 'Aurea' barberry gleam in the sun-dappled area of this shade garden. *Left:* A pink form of *Oxalis*, or wood sorrel, makes a handy—and colorful—groundcover for shady spots. *Right:* A vine-covered arbor shades rustic steps leading from the driveway to the house. Yellow primroses and hostas, tucked into the stairway, bring the quiet path to life.

embrace shade

Under a canopy of nearly 50 trees, this suburban St. Louis yard blooms with interest thanks to its design.

A mosaic of nearly 50 shade and ornamental trees throws shadows across this small lot in a community outside St. Louis. As guests stroll along the winding paths in the backyard, they come across benches and chairs tucked beneath the many canopies. Sunlight filters through the trees here and there, creating a playful mix of sun and shade. Embrace the beauty of shade with these techniques for creating a fresh, energetic garden in the shadows.

■ Be bold. The many different foliage textures can overwhelm a shade garden. The canopy of shade trees combined with dense shrubs and low-growing perennials leaves visitors' eyes questioning what to focus on. The owners of this small garden solved the problem by including bold white arbors that direct attention to key design elements, including a silky smooth urn fountain in the side garden and carved lava balls in the moss garden.

Above: The formal garden features water bubbling from a giant pot encircled by boxwood shrubs. *Right:* Looking across the garden, visitors get an entirely different perspective on the same fountain.

Above: **Rich in texture, ferns thrive in the shade.**
Left: **Clematis and roses drape over one of five benches in the small backyard. The thoughtfully placed benches sit along the many garden paths.**

■ Highlight the garden with white and pastel hues. Silver, white, and pastel flowers and leaves act like little spotlights in the garden. They brighten dark corners and complement the subtle beauty of green plants. Check out this principle at work in the urn garden, where silver-leaf dusty miller (*Senecio cineraria*) grows alongside the boxwood hedge, highlighting its lovely curve.

■ Create gathering places. Perfect for hosting summertime get-togethers, a shade garden is often 10 degrees cooler than the surrounding full-sun landscape. Capitalize on Mother Nature's air-conditioning by placing inviting benches, chairs, and tables under your favorite leafy canopy and having your friends and neighbors over for a summer soirée.

woodland wonder

Five miles outside St. Louis, a century-old home and woodsy landscape filled with natural country charm offer an escape from the city.

Left: Perky purple *Allium* 'Globemaster' adorns this garden, adding to the monochromatic color palette. Allium also gives vertical accents when planted among low-growing plants and mosses. *This photo:* This woodsy landscape with a natural slope lends itself perfectly to the trickling waterfall and stream that blend in with natural elements of this garden space. Aged wood, rock, and creeping plants give the water feature the appearance that it has always been part of the landscape.

Left: A path flanked with colorful blooms leads visitors to the rustic house and side greenhouse. The woodsy atmosphere gives the home a lodge-style feel. *Above:* Weathered birdhouses, rustic watering cans, and planters accent a potting shed overflowing with blooms and new plantings. A seating area offers a place to relax near a placid pond.

A tree-filled backyard with lush green plants, stone paths, terraces, and a trickling stream can be your escape from the bustle of everyday life. This woodland landscape is natural and free-growing but not overgrown, enhancing the beauty of nature and wonder of adventure without being overly fussy. Surrounded by 70-foot cypress trees, the garden has privacy and seclusion, lending itself to both exploration and relaxation. Here's how to plan your own woodland wonder.

■ Let nature thrive. Emphasize a free, natural look in your woodland garden by repeating elements. By strategically placing wood, stone, moss, and leafy textural plants, you can achieve a natural look. When several elements combine, each seems as if it has been there for years. A woodland garden lets plants grow freely without bounding or clipping them with strict fences or edging. In this garden, plants and moss grow through the cracks of rock walls and sandstone paths without being invasive.

This photo: Textured foliage of chartreuse and burgundy coleus fills a metal bucket, accenting a bistro table and chairs. For vibrant combinations, consider golden creeping Jenny (*Lysimachia nummularia* 'Aurea'), Wave petunias, sweet potato vine, and strobilanthes. *Right:* A vintage bike filled with seasonal plantings adds rustic charm to the backyard garden.

■ Build a water feature or stream, adding to the natural atmosphere and style of a woodland garden. Accent the waterscape with aged and mossy wood, and let plants trail into the water, or place containers for added punches of color.

■ Get creative. Combine tropicals and annuals for vivid color combinations that pop. For example, pair coleus or sweet potato vine with hibiscus. Varieties of foliage and color combinations make great focal points and fill in when some plants stop blooming later in the season.

■ Accent with rustic and country charm. Spread weathered pieces around the garden to emphasize the rustic and natural air of the space. Over time, a structure or building will earn its mossy shingles or siding and fit right into the woodsy landscape.

going all out

Create a riot of tone and texture in your garden by making it all about the foliage.

This photo: Formal urns provide unusual accents in a garden given over to foliage. A container brings agave's spiny leaves to eye level. *Right:* The leaves of this caladium set a color palette that continues in the unobtrusive flowers of the globe amaranth.

A garden dominated by foliage texture and color usually creates a quiet and reflective outdoor space. But you can make your foliage-theme garden shout "look at me," as this Atlanta landscape does, if you really go all out. Here's how:

■ Go for the green. And gold. And gray. These are all colors, although gardeners often treat them as mere scene setters. Many plants have foliage of gray, gold, and green—some as dark as night and others nearly white. Even plain old green can be as varied as chartreuse and forest. Plant families often include a variety of leaf color. Hosta leaves, for example, range from deep green with a blue cast to bright gold, yellow, and white. Many favorites have been bred to boast bold new leaf colors.

Pile on the texture. Once you've chosen a color scheme, keep the foliage theme rolling with lots of interesting shapes and textures. Notice how this garden sets up a rich interplay of form and texture. Different spaces showcase the gigantic leaves of a banana plant and the open palm leaves of the castor bean plant. Boxwoods lend a bushy feel to the edges of plantings while making living walls for beds and borders.

Vary by variegation. Pick varieties with variegated leaves to get a two-tone effect in the same plant. Or put different varieties of the same plant side by side, changing only the coloration to add visual interest and a playful feel.

Provide a place to sit among the plants. The effects of a foliage-driven garden are sometimes subtle. It takes a while for the plan to sink in, so provide a place for people to linger and notice what's going on. In this garden, weathered wooden chairs and a bistro set painted a quiet yellow are a perfect match with the color and texture of the surrounding plants.

Above: A bistro set provides a place for people to linger and get to know the garden better. *Opposite:* Foxglove, boxwood, and castor bean make a colorful combination in this corner, even though the primary color is green.

Above: **A limestone finial sits at the edge of a path. It seems to push the surrounding foliage out into the walkway, inviting people to stop and look.** *Opposite:* **The texture theme continues in this dead tree that now sprouts birdhouses instead of leaves.**

■ Make it intimate. If you expect garden visitors to pick up on the subtleties of a foliage garden, you must bring the plants in close. Pot plants in containers and set them at eye level so textures can be seen and touched. Let plants grow into paths and intrude into sitting areas. Put plants that can survive being walked on between and around your pavers and stepping-stones so your friends will get to know them as well as you do. Also, place tall plants with intriguing leaf colors and textures at the back of borders so people have to lean in to see them better. That way, your garden will have a better chance of actually touching someone.

formal
elegance

Boxwood hedges and
symmetrical paths set a
stunning framework for these
charming gardens.

rooted in history

Formal lines and classic garden style grow with abandon in this historic South Carolina garden.

The landscape surrounding this home in historic Old Charleston took root nearly 200 years ago. Time has not been kind to the half-acre property. Upon moving in, the current owners were greeted with mere remnants of a once resplendent garden. With attention to detail and respect for the past, they restored the garden's classic style. Just as it is possible to restore a home to its original grandeur, derelict gardens can also be revived by following these suggestions.

■ Visit living history. Begin restoring a garden by visiting local historic sites. Note the hardscape materials that are used, how the garden is laid out, how the plants are combined, and which plants are used frequently. Most likely, gardens in the area contained similar

Above: Laid out in a paisley shape and defined with boxwood, the rose garden spotlights David Austin rose cultivars. A circa-1880 Celtic cross serves as the focal point for the Noisette roses that are rich with Charleston history. *Right:* 'Natchez' crape myrtles perfume the garden with clouds of white flowers. Crape myrtles are used throughout the garden to tie the many garden rooms together.

This photo: Lavender-hue butterfly bush standards accent the carriage-house garden's green and white palette.
Inset: Designed to be enjoyed from above as well as from ground level, the garden has crisp, clean lines, thanks to tidy boxwood hedges.

Above: Urns planted with spiky dracaena denote the entrance to the two-tone green and white garden.
Left: Neatly clipped boxwood hedges line the cobblestone driveway. Graceful crape myrtles echo the amethyst color accents throughout the calming garden.

elements. Historic home museums are often good sources for landscaping information.

■ Find old photographs. Research the garden under renovation. Search out previous owners, and inquire about old photographs of the site. Ask neighbors whether they remember what once grew in the space. If there is a question about the original property lines, check with your local municipality about old land records.

■ Go to the library. There are many well-written books on historic landscaping. Look for ones that detail the time period to which you are working to restore your garden.

■ Call on a professional. A landscape architect can shed light on landscape styles in your area as well as assess the remnants of the landscape and suggest original elements for the space.

simple
geometry

Clean-line symmetry combines with bright white blooms to create an air of relaxed formality in this dynamic garden.

Sometimes it is hip to be square. Just take a look at this lively Kansas garden, organized around crisp square beds laid out on a horticultural checkerboard. Here's how to easily duplicate this formal look, which features a surprisingly simple design.

■ Situate the squares. Eight squares separated by pea-gravel paths form the front garden, with the porch serving as the ninth square. The backyard includes six squares, one of which is a water garden.

■ Choose one or two colors. This color palette is limited to white and green. Daffodils bloom in spring under a canopy of whitebud trees. Snow-white peonies flower in May, and pale daylilies and Japanese anemones take turns through summer and fall. Annual pansies, alyssum, vinca, and silver-edge ornamental kale fill the backyard beds under crab apples and pines.

Right: A line of offset stepping-stones leads to this front yard garden. Boxwoods trimmed into tidy cubes accent the square beds, while a rusty metal sculpture—continuing the cube theme—balances on one corner. *Above:* A water garden sparkles at the center of the backyard, which features a grid of gravel paths. Formality reigns in the planting beds, with an exclusively white and green color scheme.

Repeating elements throughout a garden establishes cohesiveness. In this back yard space, clipped boxwood hedges and concrete borders define the square beds and help unify the garden. Even within the limited color scheme of white and green, a mix of textures and leaf forms creates contrast and enlivens the space.

This photo: A pink, purple, and white cottage-style planting border creates pleasing contrast to the neatly sculpted patio plantings and lawn. *Left:* Add whimsy to any garden with spider flower *(Cleome hassleriana).* This easy-to-grow annual will reseed and pop up year after year throughout the garden.

stately
grace

Design elements borrowed from grand European gardens sculpt the landscape around this Tudor-style house in Connecticut.

Above: Enclosed by a brick wall and wrought-iron fence, the cloistered main garden takes on an air of formality. Achieve a similar feel by surrounding your garden with a tidy evergreen hedge. *Left:* Flagstone used for walls, steps, and edgings imbues a garden with a sense of permanence.

A European getaway is as close as the back door of this suburban Connecticut home. The homeowners can escape to the Victorian strolling garden after a long day at work or host a garden party amid the fragrant sprigs of lavender in the tidy herb garden. Plant a little European flair in your landscape with these simple design techniques. Soon you'll immerse yourself in the luxury of a grand estate garden on a manageable scale for today's fast-paced life.

■ Wrap a wall around your landscape. Great European gardens were walled out of necessity. While livestock no longer traipse through suburban gardens, a wall will define the space and offer a sense of enclosure. If it discourages marauding deer, all the better. A fence of brick and wrought iron encloses this garden. Achieve a similar look for less by planting a living wall. Conifers, such as juniper, arborvitae, and many varieties of spruce and pine, offer pleasing texture and year-round enclosure.

■ Create beds with strong lines. Exacting geometry defines many European estate gardens. Get a similar look with geometric planting beds. Think rectangles, squares, and circles. Define the bed edges with stone or brick borders, or use a sharp spade to cut definite edges. Neatly clipped shrubs, such as boxwood and juniper, will add to the geometric feel of a space.

■ Add old-world accents. Urns, fountains, and sculptures of all sizes are prominently displayed in many estate gardens. These pieces are used judiciously though; often one accent piece per space. For an authentic look at a fraction of the cost, look for quality reproductions at flea markets and garden centers. Constructed of weather-resistant materials such as resin, the reproductions withstand the elements and can often be left in the garden year-round.

soft-focus
formality

Going formal usually puts the
emphasis on straight lines and
square corners. This garden
seeks the softer side by
knocking off the hard edges.

Above: This patio area achieves a
level of sophistication without falling
over into stuffiness. Usually
associated with cottage style, white
Adirondack chairs settle nicely into a
seating area with a formal feel.
Clipped boxwoods swoop and curve
throughout, while yellow daylilies
brighten the plantings without
overpowering. *Left:* The white and
French blue of the surrounding
structures contrast with the green in
the plantings. Green grows between
the pavers and is layered from the
ground up. Ivy nestles at the base of
boxwoods and twines up the trees.
Hostas and hydrangeas fill out the
green theme.

This photo: Yews clipped into curves reminiscent of octopus tentacles create planting pockets for salvia. Yellow daylilies provide a counterpoint to the green and blue tones.
Right: Flowers usually associated with cottage style temper the formal lines of the garden. Yellow and orange lilies are backed by daisies, which in turn gain context from a tall backdrop of hollyhocks. Mixing informal plantings into an essentially formal garden plan offers lots of fun surprises.

Creating an eye-catching combination of formal and informal elements in a garden can be much more of a challenge than picking a particular style and playing by the rules. Playing by the rules can be boring, though; think of how much more fun it will be when you've coordinated styles.

This doesn't have to be hard; it's all a matter of balance. Once you've decided which is going to dominate, all you have to do is choose counterpoints from the other style. Here's how:

■ Paint can introduce color into a planting scheme that relies heavily on green. Use white for fences, gates, or arbors to set off the greens. If you want to feature showy cottage blooms, keep the color palette simple in the sea of green. Yellows work well in an otherwise green garden, as do blues and purples. Use oranges or reds sparingly; keep the more riotous colors for use as exclamation points in a serene space.

Clipped boxwoods bring formality to any garden, and they don't have to be square to achieve that formal feeling. Curves work well, as long as they are gentle and tie in with the rest of the shapes in the garden. Keep the formal elements simple if you're going to add cottage plantings and accents.

Feel free to mix formal and cottage accents—chairs, statuary, fixtures—in the same space, as long as you have something that unifies all the pieces. Paint them the same color, let them all weather to a rustic patina, or use similar shapes to tie the effect together. Using accent pieces in pairs brings a more balanced symmetry to the garden or patio.

Above: A gate like one that might lead to a French château welcomes visitors to this Illinois garden. Opening the top half of the gate offers a glimpse of what awaits inside. *Right:* This house and garden give the impression that they could sit in the Normandy countryside of France. The effect is heightened by the blue shutters, slate roofs, and "aged" painted brick.

Once poorly sited trees and shrubs were cleared, the homeowners found plenty of room to extend their outdoor living space. The 20×40-foot swimming pool outside the master bedroom features an exposed aggregate plaster lining that gives the water a dark blue hue.

landscape
revival

Old granite and new ideas transform a tired landscape into an inviting outdoor retreat.

Seeing an Eden in the middle of poorly sited trees, scruffy shrubs, and wan outdoor gathering areas requires an optimistic attitude. It was just such an attitude that propelled the owners of this 1920s Colonial in Westbury, Connecticut, to embark on a landscape renovation that turned their 1-acre lot into a serene collection of outdoor rooms.

■ Subscribing to the idea that landscape challenges are opportunities for design, the homeowners took advantage of their sloping backyard by creating a two-level stone patio, enclosed by the house on two sides. On the upper level, a swimming pool, fireplace, and sitting area lie just outside the master bedroom. On the lower level, a dining area covered by a linden tree canopy accommodates family meals and entertaining.

■ Just off the lower patio, a reflecting pond spans the narrow strip of land between the master bedroom and garage.

■ Enclosed by buildings on two sides and neatly trimmed hedges and stone walls on the other sides, the garden has a peaceful, private atmosphere that complements the nearby entertaining spaces.

Right: **The granite-edged reflecting pool was positioned so it could be viewed from various rooms in the house. Gravel flooring and boxwood hedges complete the low-maintenance courtyard.**
Below: **Formal elements, such as trim topiaries and clean lines, dominate this landscape. The long lines of the rectangular pool draw the eye to a distant point, while layered elements create the illusion of a larger area.**

Symmetry reigns in the courtyard with a gable-roof garage opposite the house and balanced plantings. The simple palette of green and white evokes serenity.

tropical
flair

Colorful blooms and lush foliage instantly transport homeowners and guests to another world. Peek inside to find inspiration for your own tropical getaway.

bold and beautiful

Often the best elements of an exuberant landscape are those that whisper like soft tropical breezes rather than roar like a hurricane.

Above: Planters on columns elevate what otherwise might be ho-hum plantings. Try this in your garden if you're not getting enough height from your plants to create that "palm trees swaying in the breeze" look you were going for.
Left: The giant leaves of a banana plant give any garden instant tropical flavor. But bananas are not for every climate or for every gardener. In colder climates, you can grow them in a pot or dig them up and take them inside for the winter. An easier solution might be cannas, which grow tall in a single season and come in a range of colors and variegations.

For many, the tropics don't exist only in faraway places. Most people can get there in their imaginations anytime they want—which is especially appealing on those extra busy days. So why wait? Transform that patch of grass you call a backyard into a tropical hideaway with a few well-chosen plants, a little water here and there, and a splash of paint.

■ Water should be an element in any tropical garden, but it doesn't have to be a jungle torrent or an island cascade to add a bit of paradise to your yard. Think quiet pools reflecting blue skies or a satin-smooth pond surface broken only by koi or goldfish occasionally rising to the surface.

■ You can have tropical plants—at least tropical-looking plants—wherever you live. Sure, it will be easier where the weather is warm

Opposite: In this garden, water is used in small amounts scattered throughout the landscape. Here a water lily garden in a pot sits near a fountain that spills into a pond. *Above:* A little paint in tropical hues sets off a screen and a simple concrete planter. If all that tropical foliage has you seeing too much green, paint something! *Right:* This urn—with the inside painted black to enhance reflections in the still water—becomes an instant tropical water feature.

year-round or in a climate where you get lots of moisture from a nearby ocean and your banana tree can stay in the ground. One way to get the tropical look if you don't live in a tropical climate is to use summer bulbs. Cannas are the perfect "look at me, I'm tropical" plant and can be grown just about anywhere, as long as you dig the bulbs each fall and set them out again in the spring. Dahlias, caladiums, and elephant's ear are other choices that bring their own tropical style.

■ For a really quick trip to the tropics, grab a brush and a bucket of paint. Paint a pillar Caribbean blue, make a container sunset orange, or splash yellow along a dreary wall for instant island happiness.

Above: This cosmic egg in a tropical terra-cotta color is cracked open to reveal a dark pool of water inside. A tropical garden should include quiet surprises such as unexpected water elements and twisting paths that reveal hidden treasures. *Right:* Can't grow gunnera where you live? Opt for leaves cast from concrete, which can be found in many stores and catalogs that sell outdoor accents. In this garden, a golden gunnera leaf adds drama beneath an arbor supported by weathered columns.

tropical paradise

No matter where you live, you can add a touch of the tropics to your garden and feel as if you're in paradise.

Above: Soft pink plumeria 'Jean Moragne' is a fitting contribution to this tropical garden—it's the Hawaiian lei flower. The iconic flower lines the pool and adds a light tone against the dark slate. *Right:* Palms frame the impressive lagoon-style pool and spa, while raised planters filled with bougainvillea, plumeria, and cycads place bursts of color at the pool's edge.

This photo: Water tumbles over lava-like rocks and into the pool. Plants in varying shades of green accent the soft nature of the waterfall. *Right:* The curved design of the pool, spa, and waterfall contrasts with the jagged texture of the slate and rocks encasing the elements.

Exotic plants have a certain allure. Maybe it's their spiky fronds. Maybe it's the tantalizing array of colors. Or maybe it's simply that their look conjures images of a faraway island retreat. Whatever the case, introducing tropical flair to your garden adds big personality and variety. This San Diego paradise combines several elements to achieve a truly exotic character. The spa and lagoon pool are peaceful backdrops for an abundance of plants, while island-inspired garden furniture provides an ideal spot for taking it all in.

Creating your own paradise is surprisingly easy, regardless of locale.

■ Find a way to incorporate water. The gentle sound of splashing water is calming and creates a junglelike atmosphere. While this garden boasts an expansive lagoon—complete with waterfall and spa—small-scale elements can have a similar effect. Let a small waterfall or fountain set the tropical scene in a compact space.

Opposite: Visitors are welcome to sit in the shade under the thatched palapa umbrella. Chaise longue chairs in ocean blue are inviting spots to enjoy the tropical scenery. *Right:* Plants with rich, vibrant shades—such as this jewel-tone Persian shield *(Strobilanthes dyerianus)*—add an exotic touch to any landscape.

■ Work within your zone. This mild Zone 10 garden is well-suited for exotic blooms. Naturally, plants that grow easily in California or Hawaii may be a challenge in Wisconsin. The good news: Certain varieties of tropical plants can endure temperatures into the teens. Some palms and bamboos fall into this category, including saw palmetto *(Serenoa repens)*, windmill palm *(Trachycarpus fortunei)*, and golden bamboo *(Phyllostachys aurea)*. Another option is to choose plants that can withstand the cold but appear tropical, such as Empress tree *(Paulownia tomentosa,* Zone 5), staghorn sumac *(Rhus typhina,* Zone 3), and tree of heaven *(Ailanthus altissima,* Zone 4).

■ Make the most of secondary elements. Your lounge chairs may not be the main focus in your garden, but with cool tones, they can add a subtle layer to your tropical theme. The same concept applies to umbrellas, tables, and even the materials used for walkways. In this garden, dark artificial rocks in the pool resemble lava outcroppings, while a tiki-style umbrella creates a waterside dining area.

Above: A golden orange bromeliad *(Aechmea blanchetiana)* between the waterfall and spa resembles a bonfire and adds a burst of color. *Left:* With a delicate yet intriguing shape, the Hong Kong orchid tree *(Bauhinia x blakeana)* is an interesting contrast to the garden's lancelike palm fronds. *Opposite:* Three shades of slate and tall royal palms *(Roystonea oleracea)* provide a mix of textures that surrounds the resortlike lounging area.

This photo: A mirror-backed lion fountain holds pride of place in the garden, surrounded by 'Paul's Glory' hosta, boxwood cones, and purple petunias in hanging baskets.
Left: A living headband of sedum disguises a crack in this funky gargoyle fountain.

push the limits

Tender shrubs and perennials grow alongside hardy plants in this garden that bursts with a decidedly exotic feel.

The gardeners who tend this Seattle plot regularly disregard the zones listed on plant tags. Developed to inform buyers where the plants are reliably hardy, zone distinctions have a way of reining in even the most adventurous gardeners. That's not the case here. Through trial and error and a few proven tactics, the gardeners mastered the art of growing plants that normally thrive only in warmer climates. The result is a lush urban oasis with a touch of the tropics.

Above: The garage wall serves as a backdrop for columnar apples, dahlias, lilies, canna, and a red banana, which moves indoors in winter. *Opposite:* An arbor cloaked with brilliant chartreuse hops frames a view of the checkerboard garden, which was created with inexpensive red and black pavers.

■ Move out. Add a quick tropical touch to your garden with houseplants. Croton, schefflera, pothos, and many other houseplants thrive outdoors in the summertime. Leave them in pots and tuck them into beds and borders, or group the tropicals with other container plants. For success, be sure to place them in their desired amount of light and provide adequate water. Move houseplants into their garden home when temperatures are consistently above 60°F at night. Move them inside in late summer to avoid early frosts. Be prepared for vigorous growth during summer; you'll nearly always take in a bigger plant than you moved out in spring.

■ Get a jumpstart. Many tender plants require a long growing season to flower and fruit. Wake them up early in the season by potting them and growing them in a sunny window until the last chance of frost has passed. This growing method works especially well with dahlias. Plant dahlia tubers in well-drained potting soil

mix 6 to 8 weeks before transplanting outside. Place the pot in a sunny window and water regularly. Soon shoots will emerge, followed by leaves. When all chance of frost has passed, transplant the young dahlias into the garden. They will bloom several weeks earlier than tubers that are planted directly into the garden.

■ Devise a microclimate. Courtyards, alcoves, and even densely planted shrub borders have the ability to cut biting winds, maintaining temperatures a few degrees warmer than nonprotected areas nearby. These warm niches are examples of microclimates. Plants that thrive in a zone warmer than your growing zone are likely to grow with gusto in a microclimate.

water world

You can water a garden too much, but can you have too much water in a garden? If you're talking water features, this landscape is evidence that the answer to that question would be an emphatic "no."

Above: A sense of place informs everything about this Hawaiian garden. The tall bamboo, the wide steps set into a luxurious lawn, and the Polynesian-style accents of the torches and lighting complement the home's architecture and setting. Choose plants and decorative details to enhance the space around your home, not compete with it.

Opposite: If you're considering a pond just off a porch, think about living life on the edge—of the water, that is. Bringing the pond right up to the living space means you get to fully enjoy the water garden without leaving your chair.

This photo: **This garden enhances its tropical setting by incorporating a natural-looking pool into the landscape.** *Above right:* **You can create a tropical look even if you don't have a spectacular view. Put tropical plants beside your pool, in containers if necessary. If you live in a climate that is less than tropical, move the container plants to a sheltered place when you close down the pool for the season.**

"Tropical" and "water garden" are terms that each elicit smiles from gardeners. When they are combined, smiles turn into mile-wide grins, and gardeners can't wait to dream about the results.

Those dreams can come true, even if you're a gardener who lives where tropicals are nipped by the first taste of frost. Water gardens, properly constructed, are fine for freezing climates. Make tropical plants portable by growing them in pots that can be moved inside before the snows come, or plant suitable substitutes.

■ It's all in the timing. Outdoor plants can come in, and indoor plants can go out. Grow foliage plants outdoors that you can dig and store for the winter. Fancy-leaf caladiums and similar plants are perfect for the dig-and-store style. Many tropical houseplants would love to live outdoors in the summer, if given light shade to protect them from the sun. Schefflera, mother-in-law's tongue (*Sansevieria trifasciata*), and spider plant (*Chlorophytum comosum*) are plants that thrive when given just such treatment.

■ Create a tropical backdrop. Hardy bamboos and tall ornamental grasses make perfect, almost instant, backgrounds for a tropical water garden look. Bamboo and grasses will add action to your water feature as they sway in the slightest breeze, making their reflections dance across the surface of the water.

■ You can carry the tropical look too far. If you're in a typical suburban setting, a tropical water feature in the middle of an expanse of lawn might look as if it were dropped from an alien spaceship. Be sure to integrate the water feature into a landscaped backyard, and surround it with suitable touches so it won't look out of place.

Above: A Japanese water basin fashioned from stone introduces even more water into this garden. It creates a shimmering reflecting pool, and its softly curving lines are the perfect complement to the dipping leaves of a red-violet bromeliad *(Nidularium)*. *Opposite:* A Japanese stone lantern gracefully accents the water lily leaves' flat circles. A backdrop of palms offers Asian tranquility.

front yard focus

Boost curb appeal and welcome guests in style with lush flowerbeds, an inviting walkway, or a formal courtyard near your home's main entrance.

festive entrance

This Southern California courtyard ushers guests to the front door in color-drenched style.

This photo: A cozy patio table provides ample seating for moonlit meals in the courtyard. The surrounding brick wall shields the patio from the busy street. *Right:* A basket of impatiens adds a splash of color near the wall.

A well-designed entry garden graciously welcomes guests to your home. The secret to success is to create a look that complements your house and then carry that look from the curb to the front door. An intricately painted doorbell on the outside wall inspired the colorful theme in this California courtyard. The colors and Spanish flavor of the doorbell repeat throughout the welcoming space. Create a striking garden near your front door with these simple tips.

■ Establish focal points. An arbor is a classic accent for the start of a path, but it also might frame the final destination. Blooming plants draw the eye when they're in season, but for year-round interest, consider a brightly

Above: **Numerous pots of plants decorate the length of this interior courtyard wall.** *Right:* **This patio table, a bistro table, and two seating areas make the courtyard a valuable outdoor room.**

Above: Set into the wall, this small lion's head fountain fills the courtyard with water music. A lofty ivy-filled trellis extends the height of the wall a few feet. *Left:* Masses of bright pink petunias and impatiens augment the trailing white bacopa *(Sutera cordata)* around an old olive tree.

painted door with a matching mailbox or stately urn. If your walkway or stoop is narrow, "plant" a stylish pot in a flower border for additional vertical interest.

■ Upgrade paving. Change concrete to stone or brick, and widen a narrow walkway. If your budget doesn't allow a total change, introduce new materials via a decorative edge, or cut out sections of concrete and insert decorative bands.

■ Add lighting. Don't forget what your entry looks like at night. Well-designed lighting enhances the safety and visual appeal of your landscape after dark. By day, stylish fixtures double as sculptural elements.

This photo: This Atlanta
home's location on a corner
lot suggested an updated
landscape design that
would accommodate front
and side entries from public
sidewalks. Left: A straight
path leads directly from the
street to the front door of
the painted-brick cottage.
Before a single brick could
be laid in the walkway, an
old lawn had to be torn out.

a
winning
entry

An Atlanta cottage comes
alive when a color-rich garden
replaces a tired front lawn.

Gardening in a front yard has so many advantages, it is a wonder that gardens are often hidden behind the house. A lush garden adds pizzazz to the front of a house and beautifies the neighborhood. Front yards often lack play structures, pools, and other gardening obstacles. What better way is there to greet a guest than with a billowing perennial garden?

Once a dull expanse of turf and a few foundation shrubs, this front yard in Atlanta no longer has a lawn at all. All the grass was removed, and in its place is a horticultural symphony of color and texture. The garden's tidy picket fence and walkways are tempered by cottage-style planting beds where the plants mingle freely. Here's how the gardeners created their unique mix of informal and formal style.

■ The garden has a traditional design based on a straight line drawn from the street to the front door, providing the framework for a foursquare plan. The primary paths that form the main axes are paved with old bricks. Secondary paths are carpeted with pea gravel for contrast.

■ Symmetry reigns supreme and lends a sense of order to the boisterous plantings. Four main beds are created by intersecting walkways. Each bed is anchored in its center by a tree-form hydrangea. Beyond the foursquare planting beds are rectangular plots offering additional space for pass-along plants that the homeowner gathered from her mother's and grandmother's gardens.

■ The garden contains many old-fashioned favorites such as snapdragon, larkspur, and clematis. The annual plants self-seed and eventually pop up all over the garden. Extra seedlings are easy to pluck out where they are not wanted, but those that remain add to the cottage charm and lush appearance.

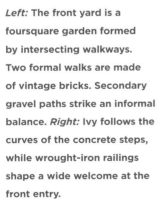

Left: **The front yard is a foursquare garden formed by intersecting walkways. Two formal walks are made of vintage bricks. Secondary gravel paths strike an informal balance.** *Right:* **Ivy follows the curves of the concrete steps, while wrought-iron railings shape a wide welcome at the front entry.**

front & center

Above: Extending from the front porch, visible in the background, to the curb, this front-yard garden is filled with annuals, perennials, small shrubs, and trees. Once a sprawling patch of grass, the bevy of front-and-center blooms regularly stops passersby in their tracks as they take in the flowering fiesta. **Right:** Planted in informal terraces cobbled together with pieces of salvaged flagstone, yellow alyssum *(Alyssum saxatilis)* and *Penstemon grandiflorus* bloom with abandon in summer. Drought-tolerant plants, they thrive with little supplemental water.

Dress up the view of your home, brighten your neighborhood, and enjoy a blooming entry with a front-yard garden. Mix in low-maintenance plants, and gardening out front is a cinch.

Roll back your green grass carpet and transform your front yard into a front garden. This might sounds like a daunting challenge, but take heart. A little planning and a love of plants will go a long way in creating a blooming entry.

Begin with a plan. Create a sketch of what your front landscape might look like when it is finished. Be sure to include walkways, patios, and other features that will make your front space functional and beautiful. This plan will change over time, but it is a vital starting point.

■ Choose site-appropriate plants. If water is a scarce resource in your area, plant drought-tolerant annuals and perennials. If clay soil is a factor, select plants that thrive in mucky conditions. Simply match plants to your growing site.

Opposite: **A water garden, consisting of an old terrazzo sink planted with water-loving plants, adds liquid refreshment to a quiet corner. Blue flax *(Linum perenne)* and blue oat grass *(Helictotrichon sempervirens)* grow in front. *Above:* Low-growing plants and a stand of Mexican feathergrass *(Stipa tenuissima)* soften the flagstone patio in the center of the garden. *Right:* The long, rectangular front yard is divided into garden rooms united by stone pathways and patios. This shady pergola is an outdoor living room perfect for taking in views of the garden.**

welcome
walkway

Greet visitors with a petal-packed
welcome mat that leads them down
the garden path, through a symphony
of vivid blooms, to your front door.

Above: Think pink. Two cultivars of argyranthemum pump up the pastel power of
the spring flower spectacular. The subtle blend of textures engages the eye, adding
visual interest to the monochromatic scene. *Right*: Nothing could be more inviting
than a charming brick path lined with blooms. In this front-yard cottage garden, spiral
junipers and pots of horsetail, an aquatic perennial, frame the front door, which also
boasts a hanging planter to greet guests.

Too often, beautiful blooms seem sentenced to spend their lives as wallflowers, stuck in a backyard garden for few to see. But at this West Coast home, flowers stand front and center, staging a grand performance that everyone within eyeshot can enjoy. You, too, can transform your front yard into a not-so-secret garden.

■ Choose a garden style that complements the style of your home. In this case, the controlled chaos of a cottage garden looks lovely next to a brick bungalow.

■ Line a walkway with overflowing borders to welcome guests and soften the linear facade of the house.

■ Mix and match blooms for a wonderfully eclectic cottage look. Airy spider flower (*Cleome hassleriana*) and daisylike argyranthemum mix magically with the papery petals of Iceland poppies (*Papaver nudicaole*). A variety—and abundance—of flowers also means bushels of blooms stand ready for cutting. It's like having a floral shop in your front yard.

■ Think year-round visual interest as you plan a front-yard garden. When one flower wanes, have another waiting in the wings to take the spotlight. Let pastel spring blooms give way to vivid summer flowers, then have orange and red blossoms take over in the fall. In this garden's mild winters, cool-season annuals and perennials flourish.

■ Spice your garden with a hint of fragrance. Basil (*Ocimum basilicum*) and fernleaf yarrow (*Achillea filipendulina*) add fresh, herby scents to top off the garden's sensory wonders.

Left: An Adirondack chair extends an invitation to stop and smell the roses—and all the other blooms in this garden room, punctuated by a run of weathered white picket fence. Classic urns and other large containers fill the brick patio with bursts of welcome color, while large trees spread cooling shade over the entire scene.

Left: An ordinary galvanized metal pail looks stunning when it brims with extraordinary plantings. Vary plant heights and textures—in addition to colors—for the most striking effect with your container gardens. They're a simple way to brighten a plain picnic table or other seating area in a cottage garden. *Below:* This midcentury brick cottage puts its best face forward, thanks to the blooms that ring it with color. The blooms spill into a pair of gardens lining the brick walk that leads to the front door. A white-painted picnic table suits the cottage style and offers an inviting perch beneath a shady magnolia tree. *Right:* Biennial foxglove (*Digitalis* spp.) brings a generous jolt of height and color. The handsome, self-seeding plant is suited perfectly to flower borders.

step on up

Terraces and steps turn an imposing sloped front yard into an easy-to-navigate flower-filled entry.

Perched on top of a mighty hill, this home in suburban Chicago posed a challenge shared by many homeowners: what to do about a steep, sloping front yard. The homeowners found an eye-pleasing solution in stone. Here's how to tame a slope and create a stunning garden.

■ Design a series of low limestone terraces that hold back the hill and create flat expanses for planting perennials. In this garden, zigzagging limestone steps climb the hill. A meandering path helps minimize the size of the house, which is a dominant landscape element at the top of the hill, by drawing attention with plantings along the way. Artful lanterns illuminate the path, making it safe to traverse day or night.

■ Plant a palette of color for blooms throughout the growing season. Purples, yellows, whites, and the occasional orange fill these terraces with color. Low-maintenance bloomers such as yarrow, lavender, and daylilies are easy-to-grow plants that rarely require deadheading or supplemental watering. Equally easy-to-grow groundcovers soften the long terraces by cascading over the edges.

Opposite: With low stacked-stone retaining walls holding the slope, this suburban front yard appears to emerge from the limestone. The multilevel house sits comfortably at the crest of the plantings. *Above:* Perennial plantings include iris, thyme, and sedum. They clamber along the stone pathway, contrasting with its hard edges and light color. Evergreen mugo pines and dwarf azaleas dot the way. *Right:* Broad limestone and timber steps with built-in step lighting connect the driveway and the front entry.

asian influence

Soothing water elements, natural materials, and distinctive foliage take center stage in these gardens. Step inside and let the rest of the world slip away.

Above: Gates and other entryways to Japanese gardens set the tone for the rest of the landscape and let visitors know right away that they'll be traveling to the exotic East. Focus on details, such as the roof, supports, and decoration on this gate. *Left:* Water in an Asian garden can be as subtle as a small pool in the hollow of a large rock, a simple bamboo fountain, or a stream that runs throughout the garden, such as the one pictured in this peaceful California landscape.

a touch of the east

A garden doesn't have to be all raked gravel, bamboo, and stone lanterns to capture the essence of the quiet serenity associated with a traditional Japanese landscape.

Serenity. Tranquillity. Meditation. Perfection. Those sound like impossible goals in the full-of-bustle world we live in today. Perfection isn't promised, but you can have some serenity and tranquillity in your own backyard by creating a garden with Japanese elements.

You don't even have to go overboard on the Asian style to build serenity into your home landscape. Eastern-style gardens are based on the idea of simplicity.

Every element should help the others blend into the overall theme of a Japanese garden. Include a stone lantern or a traditional half-moon bridge, but make it a small one and be sure it blends with the other garden elements.

You don't want to overdo the Japanese elements, especially those that would make your yard look freakish in the context of your neighborhood. This garden's Asian elements are hidden behind a high wall, which gives it a feeling of sanctuary and of being apart from the everyday world.

Left: This bridge evokes the half-moon bridges found in many Japanese gardens but does it in a subtle way. By incorporating a gentle arch instead of the full half-moon shape, the bridge blends with its surroundings rather than dominating them. *Top:* An in-ground spa adds to this California garden's sense of peace and relaxation. While not an element of traditional Asian style, a spa will add to an owner's sense of tranquillity with its soothing massage. A bamboo fence and artistically placed boulders bring in suitable Japanese elements.

If you're pondering a Japanese garden, consider focusing on these elements:

■ Use the basics as the touchstones for your Japanese garden: rock, water, and bamboo. Try using them in subtle yet surprising ways, and you'll have success with your Asian landscape.

■ Keep it natural. The elements you pick should look as if they've always been there. Plants should look as though they grew in place, even if they've just come from the nursery. Gates and walkways should whisper, not shout, the Japanese theme.

Left: Nothing says Japanese garden like a stone lantern and bamboo fencing. Incorporate a few traditional touches to set the theme for an Asian garden before branching out with your own design ideas. *Opposite:* A traditional bamboo waterspout with a stone basin adds the serene sound of running water to the garden. *Below:* Architectural details on the entry gate set the tone for the garden and ease visitors' transition from suburban sidewalk to Japanese paradise.

incline
opportunity

Steeped in Asian flavor, a screened house on stilts makes optimum use of a sloping yard.

This photo: The garden is serene thanks to the woodland preserved in the ravine and the gentle sound of running water. *Right:* Naturally rippled limestone slabs form a bridge and encourage visitors to slow down so they can enjoy the journey.

A steep, wooded ravine proved to be the perfect perch for this garden retreat deep in the heart of Texas. Often met with trepidation and deemed unusable, a precariously sloping yard or ravine can actually offer landscaping opportunities to gardeners who see assets where others see liabilities. With a little creative thinking and a hefty dose of hard work, this steep half-acre slope was transformed from a patch of grass and scrub into a popular outdoor gathering space. Rethink your slope situation with these tips for landscaping on an incline.

■ Take advantage of terraces. A gentle series of terraces built with native limestone creates flat expanses every few paces down this sloping backyard. Not only do terraces make it easier to climb up and down a slope, but they also provide planting opportunities.

This photo: Edged with limestone, round ponds filled with water hyacinths *(Eichhornia crassipes)* enhance the Zenlike serenity of the garden. *Left:* A pipe creates a rustic fountain, spilling water into the lower pond. The running water muffles nearby traffic noise.

■ Add water. Because water naturally runs downhill, take advantage of this rule of nature to add music to your space. A meandering stream, small waterfall, or pond-and-fountain combination are valuable liquid elements for sloped retreats. A simple recirculating pump powered by electricity will push water back up the slope.

blurring the lines

Complementary elements design a smooth transition between inner home and outdoor spaces.

This photo: A relaxed sitting area with a fireplace and a private dining area under the canopy of a yellow shade sail offer several choices for entertainment and atmosphere. *Right:* This simple grass centerpiece lends itself to the courtyard's modern look, while black-fabric casual furniture blends function and style.

Simple design joined with Asian influence copied from elements inside the home enhance the outdoor courtyard and garden of this contemporary California location. By blurring the line between the indoor and outdoor living spaces, you can extend your home into another realm. This home extension can be a restful retreat for reading or an elegant space for entertaining friends and relatives.

This garden has it all. From the meditation garden to the sleek sitting area beneath the canopy, the combination of plants and design accents blends the rooms of this outside space into a sophisticated but casual hideaway. Here's how to extend your home into the garden to get a similar look.

This photo: Bamboo and lush green living walls add texture and provide protection for meditation spaces. Large dense black pots complement the simple design and add contrast with feathery asparagus fern (*Asparagus densiflorus* 'Myersii'). *Right:* A glazed black pot creates an unexpected fountain with a bamboo spout hidden inside a wall of flowering jasmine. The sound of flowing water enhances the harmony of any meditation space.

■ Borrow and repeat elements from inside your home. By repeating lines, shapes, and colors, you create a more unified space, expanding living space beyond the walls of the home in reality and visual awareness.

■ Pick plants with texture and ones that create a monochromatic color palette. Ferns, black bamboo (*Phyllostachys nigra),* grasses, and horsetail (*Equisetum hyemale)* create solid texture. Birch, ficus, and maple trees add leafy vertical accents and canopy. For a simple color palette, plant white flowering plants. Consider star jasmine vines (*Trachelospermum jasminoides)* and white azaleas (*Rhododendron* spp.).

■ Choose bold accents and furniture that add contrast to the space. The contrast of black containers, black bamboo, and black rocks against white birch (*Betula jacquemontii)* and feathery ferns emphasize the tranquil serenity of the space.

Left: Horsetail *(Equisetum hyemale)* and black bamboo *(Phyllostachys nigra)* turn a side garden into a visual art piece formed with simple lines and balance. *Above right:* A simple centerpiece underscores the clean and sophisticated design of the space. *Below right:* Polished black rocks accent the base of a potted tree, creating contrast between the dark container and the white birch tree trunk.

now & zen

The simple beauty of nature creates a spot for peaceful retreat in this California garden.

Left: A wooden gate frames a picture of this peaceful Zen garden that invites guests to follow a stone path. Egyptian paper rush (*Cyperus papyrus*) and kangaroo paw (*Anigozanthos* 'Red Cross') border the entryway. *This photo:* A stucco wall provides protection and privacy, and defines this peaceful garden accented with traditional Japanese sculpture, a prayer bell, and stone etchings.

Bamboo fountains and stepping-stone paths lead visitors on a soul-soothing journey through this plant-filled take on a Zen garden.

Careful selection of key elements can turn a simple outside space into a serene landscape where you'll find relaxation. But given just the right twist, the same space can become the perfect place to entertain.

Plants are repeated throughout this garden to emphasize the unity of the space, and authentic Japanese accents are positioned to create scenes for meditation and contemplation. Listen and welcome harmony into your own landscape by adding a few key elements.

■ Pick a palette of plants and natural elements to repeat throughout the garden. Consider Japanese maple (*Acer palmatum*), bamboo, ferns, and Japanese boxwood (*Buxus microphylla* var. *japonica*). Accent the space with natural stone, rock, and water. Place Japanese statues of Buddha, lanterns, stone etchings, and fountains to create authenticity and picturesque vignettes along the garden path.

This photo: A typical Japanese dry stone- and-sand design can sometimes be too bare. This garden blends Japanese-style plants and accents throughout the stone river and the lush green landscape.
Right: Asparagus fern (*Asparagus densiflorus* 'Myersii') gives soft texture to the Zen garden design and contrasts with rocks and other hardscaping to create a multitude of textures.

■ Think 3D and choose a multitude of textures. Position combinations of plants for repeated texture. A textural grass or moss growing in a stone-pattern floor creates an eye-popping focal point that can emphasize natural lines and angles.

■ Draw the boundaries of your garden sanctuary with vertical accents. Garden structures and walls protect and define your outdoor space but allow the seclusion of a serene spot. Add screens, walls, arbors, and hedges to emphasize the privacy and depth of the outdoor space.

backyard
retreats

Escape to the sanctuary
of these hidden getaways
and relax in comfortable
seating areas surrounded
by abundant blooms and
refreshing water elements.

panoramic oasis

An innovative pool and spa are the centerpiece of a backyard designed for family-friendly living.

A sheltered outdoor kitchen and an umbrella-shaded sitting area overlook the pool. Shade is essential for outdoor living in Southern California, and a watering hole offers a fun, refreshing splash on hot days.

An impressive, natural-looking pool is the heart of this backyard in Carlsbad, California, but it's the smaller design features, such as landscape lighting and poolside seating, that make the landscape a favorite destination day and night. Take cues from this landscape as you craft your own backyard paradise.

■ Incorporate a pool and spa. On a stiflingly hot day, the pool's beach entry provides a place for semisubmerged lounging, and at day's end, the adjoining spa offers one of the best seats in the house for watching the sunset. Boulders artfully positioned around the perimeter of the pool complement its organic shape. The stone theme continues on the bottom of the pool, which is lined with smooth black onyx pebbles.

■ Include a covered kitchen and seating area. An outdoor kitchen sits at one end of the pool and a slightly raised seating area at the other. A small stone bridge arching over a softly flowing stream provides access to the seating area, which overlooks the pool and a neighboring canyon. On cool nights a cozy gas fireplace provides sufficient warmth.

Opposite: As an element of the backyard design, the pool provides proportion to the scheme, giving it balance. In addition to a built-in spa, the pool features a continuous-flow skimmer, a sonar-safety device (which detects unusual disturbances of the water's surface), and a saltwater chlorinator (which makes the water easy on eyes and skin). *Above:* The Southwest-inspired covered fireplace runs on natural gas. The homeowners wanted neither sparks nor smoke largely because a nature preserve is located nearby. *Right:* In the poolside garden, a stream traipses among plantings and over rocks, while its source is disguised by a tipped jar.

The backyard design features destinations organized in a series of multipurpose rooms, such as a pergola-sheltered sitting room complete with fireplace.

contemporary
vibe

Concrete blocks form
the bones of an inviting
modern landscape.

Left: A spillway, added to the entry courtyard by pouring concrete to form waterproof walls, is home to a potted variegated fortnight lily *(Dietes iridioides)*. *Below:* Before the landscape makeover, the yard was a big slope; a concrete slab provided a landing outside the house. Now a courtyard entryway leads down steps to the driveway and across stepping-stones to a gravel terrace.

Designing a garden to complement the house is always a winning strategy. If your house has a modern flavor, take cues from this well-done contemporary landscape and include these smart design elements.

■ Concrete blocks set the tone for the sloping yard in Ojai, California. The blocks were painted white and used to create a collection of raised planters and retaining walls. The smooth blocks match materials from the house itself, and the straight lines of the walls underscore the home's modern geometry.

■ Walls divide and welcome. The first wall visitors see—just 8 inches high—edges a courtyard beside the driveway. Higher retaining walls create the pea-gravel terrace that stretches along the right side of the house.

■ A terrace provides comfortable living space. Accessible via a stepping-stone path and slate-tile steps, the 20×32-foot terrace is spacious enough for hosting parties, but it's also a tranquil and intimate retreat. The entry court's spillway is visible—and audible—from a dining area in one corner. Beyond the dining terrace, a low-maintenance planting of leatherleaf sedge (*Carex buchananii*) rustles in the breeze.

Below: A bonsai-pruned mugo pine stands out against the painted-block exterior along the front entry. Sedum fills the planting bed with uncluttered beauty. *Right:* Just off the terrace, a rooftop deck above the garage extends the outdoor living area. Burro's tail (*Sedum morganianum*) that tumbles over the edge of a planter is among the spare, easy-care plantings.

Top: An army of sedges (tall, wispy *Carex buchananii* and low *Carex compacta)* marches across the terrace in a simple yet dramatic display. *Above:* Mexican feathergrass *(Stipa tenuissima)* fills planters along the front stairway, continuing the planting scheme's focus on simplicity. With plantings secondary to hard elements such as walls, terraces, and paths, this landscape design works well with the home's architecture. *Right:* This dining terrace with a pea-gravel floor brings rustic, Mediterranean flavor to the high-style, low-maintenance landscape. Terracing the hillside makes it appear larger.

kick back

Weeding and watering are tempered with ample opportunity to sit back and take in the beauty of this Washington garden.

A perfect vantage point for viewing the garden during all seasons, the back porch is outfitted with plush comforts that encourage lingering. When temperatures dip, guests wrap up in one of the many quilts and take in the scene.

Relaxing is a mandatory activity in this Bainbridge Island, Washington, garden. The inviting back porch, with a commanding view of the garden beyond, beckons, as do the occasional garden chores. Both pursuits—gardening and kicking back—are enjoyed thanks to creative garden design that minimizes maintenance and maximizes time spent enjoying the space. Make time to take in the pleasures of your Eden with these low-maintenance garden design strategies.

■ Define the garden with hardscaping and structures. Flagstone paths, cobblestone-edged planting beds, neat and tidy picket fences, and welcoming arbors form this temperate garden's foundation. The hardscape elements and structures lend the garden a formal feel and create a sense of order among the varied perennial and shrub plantings. And best of all, they require almost no maintenance.

Above: **Just off the back porch, this centerpiece bed marries formal and informal design. The easy-care bed includes boxwood, barberry, and billowy cape fuchsia.**
Right: **Golden hops and clematis clamber up an arbor leading to the kitchen garden.**

Above: **The large flowers of 'Victor Hugo' clematis intertwine with the lavender spikes of toadflax (*Linaria* spp.). *Left:* A Dutch door, rooster weather vane, windows, window boxes, and a coat of periwinkle paint turn an otherwise lackluster prefabricated garden shed into a spectacular garden focal point.**

■ Choose well-behaved plants. Some plants demand constant attention to look their best, while others strut their stuff with hardly a helping hand from the gardener. This garden is filled with the latter.

Plants that would grow too large or be unruly are not allowed. Instead loosely structured plants, such as meadow rue (*Thalictrum* spp.), toadflax (*Linaria* spp.), penstemon, and yarrow (*Achillea* spp.), fill the beds. The delicate foliage is punctuated by a few bold, structured plants, including New Zealand flax (*Phormium tenax*), neatly trimmed dwarf boxwoods (*Buxus sempervirens* 'Suffruticosa'), and a topiary arborvitae (*Thuja* spp.). A living privacy fence of flowering trees and shrubs and evergreens borders the back of the garden.

quiet reflections

Multiple seating areas and water features in this Connecticut garden encourage visitors to relax and enjoy the view.

As you step into this Connecticut backyard through the arbor covered with clematis, akebia, and wisteria, the swimming pool—complete with the essential chaise longues—slowly comes into view. Once cut off from the rest of the garden, it is now surrounded by various garden rooms and seamlessly blends into the landscape. A new patio at the far end of the house offers additional space for quiet conversations and summer entertaining. Looking around the outdoor space, it is obvious that guests are meant to stay awhile and admire the magnolias, dogwoods, and hostas from all angles. That's just how it was planned when the 5-acre property was transformed into a welcoming oasis with a few simple design strategies, which you can consider when planning your relaxing retreat.

Left: **Simple seating areas throughout the yard extend the living space outdoors.** *Above:* **A post-and-rail fence around the pool was torn out and the terrace area leveled.**

■ Focus on views from the house. Study the views from each window of the house. Add focal points in each area you can see, and improve transitions from the house to the garden to subtly blend inside and out. Here, foundation plantings reach into the yard to connect the pool with the rest of the landscape. Outside the living room, a boxwood garden with shrubs planted in a staggered pattern adds intriguing form and texture throughout the year.

■ Aim for continuity. Repeat specific elements in various areas of the garden to provide the space with a cohesive look and feel. The style of the garden bench repeats in the design of a garden gate, while traditional stone pathways and walls lend seamless character throughout this 1½-acre garden.

■ Add inviting entrances. Here's our top piece of advice: Include an entrance to the garden that doesn't go through the house. Try locating the main garden entrance at the side of the house. Here, double-lattice gates invite visitors to step into a fieldstone avenue lined with hostas. A hedge of arborvitae just inside the gate hides the pool area.

Left: **A small pond elegantly set into a bluestone patio outside the screen porch enhances indoor and outdoor views.** *Above:* **Water trickles softly into the pond, bringing the soothing sounds to the patio.**

■ Don't be afraid to make changes to the plan as you go. Maintain your straight lines, if you must, but every now and then let a new plant that's stolen your heart find its way into the mix. These slight adjustments to the overall plan only serve to make the garden more interesting—and inject it with a dash of personality.

Above: One of the high-art additions to this garden is its sculptural plants. *Aloe polyphylla* is a spiral-form succulent from South Africa. It can grow to 16 inches across. *Left*: The sculpted stairway is made with heavy timbers set into the hillside and leveled off with crushed rock. This creates a way to stroll down from a deck to a succulent garden that is made even sweeter by the fragrance of roses and lavender growing nearby.

hillside
sculpture

As surely as a human form chipped from a block of granite deserves to sit in a museum, this garden carved out of a hillside is also a work of art.

Gardeners often approach landscaping a slope as a problem to be solved. The real artist will see just more raw material to be molded into something beautiful.

Do that in your own sloping backyard by beginning with the basics and milking the details for all they're worth. Use whatever artist's cliché you want—blank canvas, lump of clay, block of marble—your task is to find the beautiful garden clinging to the side of the hill and make it real.

■ Scour your site with the best sights in mind. Take a chair—a comfortable one—and sit in various spots to savor the views. Make sure to sample the spots you would never imagine sitting. If the view is perfect, you can always build a small deck or terrace there to provide a level place for a couple of chairs and a small table. Building a path to get there just might result in all sorts of new ideas and exciting planting spots too.

Above: Carefully placed plants mask a deck that otherwise would jut over the hillside, dominating the view. Remember to consider all perspectives—from the deck down and from the ground back up again—when evaluating where to plant what.

Right: Take advantage of paths that meander down a hillside by paying attention to the vistas they create. Here the view is framed by Japanese maples and California live oaks.

■ Create destinations if you can't discover suitable ones. This California gardener planted a succulent garden after discovering that the plants would grow well on the quick-draining hillside. Consider putting a fragrant garden at the end of a winding path and letting your guests' noses guide them there. Or create a sculpture garden on a hidden terrace, and place smaller works of art along the path that leads there.

■ Find plants suitable for your particular slope. Meet this challenge by asking advice from gardeners in your area who have similar conditions.

Left: Succulent plants and a couple of fanciful sculpted chairs enliven one of the terraces created when the gardener set out to tame this hillside. Planning plantings to take advantage of their overall look and not just their blooms can add texture, color, and form to any garden. Some of the succulents used here are agave, aloe, and echeveria. *Above:* If you plan things right, you can go from having no place to sit on a hillside to having a choice of locations and views. Small wooden decks break up the slope and create centers of interest at various points on the hillside.

cottage style

Carefree blooms and vintage garden elements fill these yards with quaint charm that always delights.

in living color

Everywhere you look, cheerful color bursts from every nook and cranny in this flower-filled retreat.

Left: A charming white picket fence is flanked by a riot of color from pink bee balm (*Monarda didyma*) and lavender-color Russian sage (*Perovskia* 'Blue Spire') along one side and yellow black-eyed Susan (*Rudbeckia fulgida*), pink foxglove (*Digitalis* spp.), and a bright mix of annuals on the other. A white obelisk decorates the background of the scene. *Above:* Royal purple clematis 'The President' twines its way along most of the length of fence. The 6-inch-wide blooms cloak the span in color in late spring and summer before the vine blooms again in late summer and fall.

Left: Along the front walk, guests are greeted by a carefree border of annuals and perennials. Underfoot, they'll find blue star creeper *(Isotoma fluviatilis)* inching its way between the pavers. Up high, glimpses of color come from window boxes and vines growing along the roof and window lines.

Above: Two varieties of dahlia are joined by garden phlox *(Phlox paniculata)* in flanking a copper birdbath.

Getting your garden to bloom all at once is one thing. Keeping it blooming all season is a different story entirely. Following the tips from this brightly blooming garden, you can enjoy color from early spring well into the cool days of fall.

■ Mix it up. Choose plants with varying bloom times and growth habits. This Oregon garden is brimming with a mix of perennials, annuals, and vines that flower at various times, so something, and often more than one plant, is blooming almost all the time.

■ Snip the blooms. Many plants respond well to deadheading, a key to the long bloom time of this garden. To do this, snip off blooms that are no longer attractive. You'll not only clean up your garden, but you'll also send a message to the

plants to continue flowering, extending the bloom time for several weeks in most cases. Collecting flowers for bouquets also promotes rebloom, and you'll enjoy a bit of your garden on your table as well.

■ Think high and low. Adding color up high and down low can give the impression of lots of flowers, even when only a few are blooming. Here, colorful vines ramble up arbors and over fences, creating a pretty garden backdrop. Even after the flowers have faded, classic white structures provide a striking contrast to the green foliage.

■ Fill in with containers. Pots, baskets, and containers are portable, so use them to your advantage. Where this garden leaves off, hanging baskets, window boxes, and pots of color seamlessly fill in with hue-rich combinations.

Left: Arches in the arbor's structure provide an ideal place for hanging color up high. Comfortable garden-motif cushions line the swinging bench, making it easy to relax for a while. *Below:* Large hanging baskets of trailing annuals add impact to this garden structure. This one is filled with a mix of annuals—red verbena, white twinspur, purple petunias, and pink ivy geraniums (*Pelargonium* spp.)—that bloom all season.

charming, with class

Webster's definition of cottage garden could easily be "exuberant and fun, without ever getting out of control." Take as one example, this British Columbia garden.

Left: Tall plants, such as foxgloves and delphiniums (*Pacific Giant hybrids*), surround this cottage with lofty color. Other plants to consider for height in a cottage garden are *Nepeta* 'Six Hills Giant' and tall forms of bellflowers (*Campanula*) in white and blue. For a tall, slender look, think about using wafts of *Verbena bonariensis*. Fill in at the base of tall plants with low-growing plants that have plenty of foliage. *Above: Potentilla nepalensis* 'Miss Willmott' creates a cottage feel with its loose, sprawling growing style. Pastel colors add to the easy charm in cottage gardens.

Sometimes, rustic is a nice way to say run-down—a garden that's more shabby than chic. If that's what you think of rustic, you'll have to find another word for this British Columbia garden, such as charming or cozy or just plain beautiful.

If you're interested in creating charm in your own garden without letting it slip over into messy, try some of these tactics to keep tacky in check.

■ Stick to a theme. This garden works because it is about just one thing. It knows it's a cottage garden, so it doesn't try to be anything else. The structures are rustic. The plantings are all about old-fashioned favorites. The paths are loose, winding, and relaxed.

■ Tall is beautiful. Tall plants. Tall structures. Accents in the gable ends of the house that make it look even taller than it is. This garden is just tall, tall, tall. That reinforces its exuberance without letting everything go over the top.

■ A cottage garden should be the perfect complement to the cottage it surrounds. Cottage is sometimes overdone. It especially looks overdone in the wrong setting. Make sure that traditional cottage plants such as old roses, delphiniums, foxgloves, dianthus, and lady's mantle will work with the structures and decorative touches in the garden.

Above left: Paths don't have to lead anywhere in a cottage-style garden, but when they do, the gates and arbors that greet them should suit the relaxed mood. *Left:* Rustic tools in a rustic trug are perfect accents to a rustic garden. Use accents carefully and sparingly in a cottage design, however. The variety and sheer size of plants in this kind of garden call for restraint in decoration. *Right:* A climbing rose in soft pink transforms a simple shed into an integral part of the garden. The grasses growing on the roof top off the effect.

Left: In this free and loose garden, cottage plants grow right up against the front of the cottage—and it's OK. *Right:* The hybrid musk rose 'Buff Beauty' has large clusters of lightly fragrant double blooms that are apricot when they emerge, then fade to buff. *Below:* Roses are perfect for a cottage garden. In this border, 'Mme. Ernest Calvat', 'Maigold', and 'Alchymist' share an arbor bed with peonies, lady's mantle *(Alchemilla mollis)*, and bellflowers *(Campanula)*. Using roses that grow to different heights avoids the "soldiers in a row" look common to many rose gardens.

relaxed
attitude

Bountiful blossoms and
striking structures in this
Missouri landscape create
a gracious garden.

After entering the garden through the white arbor, visitors are enveloped in a floral embrace. Yellow daylilies, pink phlox, and pink and white coneflowers bloom in the foreground while roses, butterfly bushes, and cosmos decorate the far side of the garden.

Above: **The still tight buds flanking the open rose reveal that weeks of bloom are ahead for this bush.** *Opposite:* **Form and function meet in this arbor as it frames a pretty view of the house and provides structure for the climbing rose.**

Great cottage gardens appear to have sprung up on their own. Self-seeding plants mingle with abandon, popping up here and there to create a garden full of come-again color. At the same time, roses ramble through planting beds and over arbors while massive hydrangea hedges bow with blooms. This delightful look is achieved with a touch of happenstance and some thoughtful garden design. Here are a few design tips that will give your garden the carefree cottage look.

■ **Mix it up.** Annuals, perennials, shrubs, and small trees coexist in a cottage garden. Mix your favorite plants from each group for a striking display of color, shape, and texture. Shrubs are not typically thought of when it comes to cottage gardens, but hydrangeas have a bold presence in this one. Their good

This photo: Cool colors—purples, blues, and greens—dominate the water garden. The result is a restful retreat. *Right:* Blue flag *(Iris versicolor)* is a water iris that thrives when planted in the pond. Other irises, such as Japanese and Siberian, grow in well-drained soil along the pond's margin.

looks continue long after they finish blooming. Expect the flower heads to remain until the end of summer; many varieties sport yellow fall color.

■ Add structure with garden accents. A picket fence, a graceful arbor, or an obelisk all say cottage garden at first glance. Take advantage of the form and function of garden accents by wrapping your patch in a pleasing picket fence or framing an entry with an arbor.

■ Don't forget fragrance. For supreme enjoyment of a space, involve as many senses as possible. Enthrall the sense of smell with fragrant flowers and foliage. Old-fashioned roses perfume the garden with classic cottage smells. Lavender, thyme, basil, and many other herbs boast fragrant foliage.

Above: Surrounded by a hydrangea hedge, this moss-covered brick patio plays host to informal garden gatherings. *Left:* A wire basket containing clay pots serves as functional garden art. A pink rose climbs a trellis in the background, offering hints of welcome fragrance and color. *Right:* Water lilies and blue flags add lush plant life to the glassy surface of the oval-shape pond.

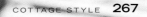

cultivated
cottage

Not wild, not mild, this garden tip-toes on the edge of estatehood while never straying too far from its obvious cottage-garden heritage.

Above: An elevated bluestone terrace provides a great overview of the garden. Make the most of potential views by placing beds, borders, planters, and statuary where they can be seen best.

Right: Keep in mind the foreground view. At the front edge of this overlook, the homeowner uses annuals in soft purples and whites to frame the garden below and complement the purple and yellow blossoms there.

No matter whether you're designing an all-out English garden or just one that borrows aspects from the Cotswolds, a few simple principles will help you create your piece of that sceptered isle.

You can't simply copy a Cotswolds cottage garden for your own estate in the states. The climate is different. The soil is different. The plant selection is different. Here's how to take elements of the English and adapt them to your particular conditions.

▪ Create borders. That's one way to keep a cottage garden in check. The problem that arises is how to keep your borders from becoming tiny strips of flowers edging a great expanse of lawn. Move the borders to center stage by creating island beds or drifts. Let the beds define their own spaces rather than letting the space define where you'll put planting beds. Let a peninsula grow from your border, and divide the lawn into smaller spaces. Or let a drift swoop around to soften a slight slope in your yard.

▪ Stick to a few kinds of flowers to unify the garden. That doesn't mean that if you like daylilies you have to have only 'Stella de Oro' daylilies. Just stay in the same plant family—or the same two or three—and you won't have a problem.

▪ Pick a color scheme and stick to it. If you start with yellows and blues, try to maintain that, except for selected departures to add punch to an otherwise boring corner.

Left: A Cotswold-style cottage looks perfectly at home among drifts of daylilies and hostas in this New Hampshire landscape. The drifts of flowers break what otherwise would be a great expanse of grass. *Above right:* These daylilies grow right down to the edge of the constructed pond on this property. If you don't have room for a full-size pond, use plants to edge a water feature of any size. *Right:* Plantings are repeated right up to the back door of this cottage. If there are no beds by your back door, consider planting in pots to dress up your gateway to the garden.

If you can't afford to buy enough plants to fill your beds and borders right away, take a tip from this homeowner and choose perennials that are easily divided. You can start with a few clumps of daylilies and hostas and, with a little digging and dividing each growing season, end up with the bounty seen here.

Left: Use gates and paths in your garden to create more than just avenues to get from here to there. Gates are opportunities to focus your visitors' attention without blocking the view. This one looks out from the extensive backyard gardens onto a front terrace. *Right:* If you have an upper-level deck or terrace, make sure you plan your plantings to fill the space. Here, trailing annuals spill over to almost meet the tall yellow daylilies growing up from below. The flowers and foliage mask what otherwise would have been a dark hole in the view. *Below:* Visitors always welcome a place to sit and enjoy your garden, especially where it is least expected. This low stool that sits beside one of the borders is nestled near a low birdbath. Even a shallow dish such as this can create an instant water feature.

simple
delights

Filled with flowers of every size and steeped in sweet fragrance, cottage gardens delight the senses. Take cues from this charmer, and get planting!

Above: An unusual combination of peach and pink bloom together in pastel beauty. 'Westerland' rose and hardy geranium 'Wargrave Pink' are two of the many colorful blooms that bedeck this garden. Cottage style is rich in color—from pastels to vibrant hues. Choose a color palette, and use it as a guide when selecting flowers. *Right:* Climbing roses 'Bleu Magenta' and *Rosa moschata* drape a wood arbor with blooms each June in this Oregon garden. Pergolas, obelisks, and arbors are excellent structures for supporting upwardly mobile roses and flowering vines.

It is easy to understand why cottage gardens are wildly popular. Who would not revel in being surrounded by spikes and spires of blooming plants from spring until first frost? Although each cottage garden bears the personal stamp of its gardener, most have common attributes that you can incorporate in your plan.

■ A free-flowing attitude. Meticulous planting plans go by the wayside in a cottage garden. Drifts of long-blooming plants ebb and flow through the garden, creating waves of color. Plants often self-sow and pop up here and there to create a crazy quilt of favorite flowers.

■ Simple and cozy retreats. Enjoy bountiful blooms in the cottage garden by tucking a bench under an arbor or clustering three chairs near a border that's bursting with bloom. Visit antiques stores and flea markets to find country-inspired chairs and benches made of wicker, wrought iron, and wood.

Above: **Easy-to-grow annuals pink mallow (*Lavatera trimestris* 'Silver Cup') and yellow California poppies (*Eschscholzia californica*) mingle in a garden bed. Encourage the duo to self-sow by not cultivating the planting area between growing seasons.**
Opposite: **Ox-eye daisies (*Leucanthemum vulgare*), catmint (*Nepeta* 'Six Hills Giant'), evening primrose (*Oenothera* spp.), and *Geranium psilostemon* add color from early summer until frost.**

inviting getaway

Inside this cozy Georgia cottage garden lives an everyday retreat filled with color.

This photo: A clean white arbor and picket fence support scrambling roses and clematis. The arbor and fence outline the garden entrance and act as the backdrop for a colorful splash of blooms in reds and pinks. *Left:* Antique birdhouses complement the rustic charm of this cottage garden and add support and structure for climbing plants to embrace and a place for birds to nest.

This photo: A charming brick path curves through the garden, shaping and defining boundaries of colorful beds. Spilling with 'Alister Stella Gray' and red 'Blaze' roses, an arbor frames a portal to the unseen garden, giving a glimpse of what lies around the corner. *Right:* Oriental poppies *(Papaver orientale)* emit the sense of a cozy, free-growing garden with vibrant punches of color and height. Poppies lend wonderment and allure to a cottage garden, presenting a bit of magical charm.

Careful cultivation and planning transformed this former pecan plantation into a rustic Victorian cottage garden. Most of the effort to turn it into a flower-filled cloister bursting with color went into soil preparation.

The same care should be taken in getting your own soil ready. After the initial preparation, you can design your theme, planting plan, and color palette. Employ each of these key elements to your advantage to set the framework for your cottage garden.

■ Choose a theme. Your theme should complement your home and landscape. Infuse the garden with accents that illustrate the rustic allure, such as antique birdhouses, farm tools, signs, and weathered furniture. Birdhouses offer wonderful accents and invite wildlife into the garden. Scatter these elements to emphasize the free-flowing atmosphere. Choose flowers with cottage charm, such as poppies, roses, clematis, snapdragons, and peonies.

Support with structure, and define with borders. Arbors, fences, trellises, and stone walls help support vertical-growing and wandering plants. This garden's white picket fence and arbor offer a clean canvas for colorful, rambling blooms to thrive. Paths and edging create borders to define the garden's shape and offer boundaries that keep plant beds from growing out of control.

Pick a long-lasting color palette. Find a color scheme that will carry your garden through the blooming season, such as that used in this red, pink, and pastel garden. The accent color unifies the garden no matter the size and emphasizes the cottage theme. Mix long- and short-blooming plants. Fill in drab spots with colorful container plantings while waiting for more blooms.

Above: Visitors can stop and smell the roses lining a split-rail fence and relax on antique-looking furniture. Charming iron fences surround the checkered grass-and-stone courtyard. These antique accents complement this Victorian cottage-style garden's charisma. *Right:* Under a pecan tree dressed in false climbing hydrangea (*Schizophragma hydrangeoides* 'Moonlight'), this space provides a place for dining and entertaining under a leafy canopy of shade. New plants find a home in a centerpiece greenhouse.

index